MEANINGFUL

A Personal Pursuit of the American Dream

Gonzalo Jimenez

www.GonzaloJimenezInsurance.com

Meaningful

By

Gonzalo Jimenez

© 2013 by Gonzalo Jimenez Insurance Agency, Inc.

ISBN: 978-0-9790036-4-6

Published by Hastings House Publishing, LLC.
www.WriteABook.us

Edited by: Cristina Adams
Book Design by: Christina Fuselli

Table of Contents

Acknowledgements

There are many people who have made me the person I am today and without them, none of this would be possible. Before I begin to tell my story, I would like to express my appreciation to each of them for their love and support.

First, I would like to thank my parents, **Gonzalo Jiménez Bejar Caballer**o and **María Yolanda Bernal Abadia**.

Even though he wasn't always there for me, my father showed me that through hard work, I could accomplish anything. My father passed away in 2009 and is with my sister **Nena** who passed away in 1966. I miss you both very much. From time to time, I can feel their presence and I know they are watching from up above.

My brother, **Dwight B. Jiménez** lives in Houston and I get to see him often. He is a successful accountant and I'm proud of his success.

My children: **Jason, Bryan** and **Gina Lee**. They are the reason I have strived day-after-day to become a better father and a

better person. Everything my wife and I have built together over 36 years of marriage has been done for them, with the goal of creating strong roots to help them grow up in this crazy world.

What's more, they have taught me many things along the way. With their entrepreneurial skills and business savvy, they have really shown me how to harness and adapt to new ways of doing business and constant innovations in technology. The results have been both successful and amazing. I would do anything for my kids: today, tomorrow and forever.

My beautiful wife, Luz Marina, is the best thing that ever happened to me. She keeps me focused and gives me emotional stability. Uniquely humble and charismatic, she is the type of person who will do virtually anything for somebody in need, whether she knows that person well or not. When I met her, she was a diamond in the rough. Now, 36 years later, she is the brightest diamond, a shining star that enhances my life the way nothing else can.

Past President and CEO of Farmers Insurance Group of Companies, **Martin D. Feinstein.** Marty was the third CEO in my career with Farmers which is the company that I have represented since 1981. He showed me how to become a leader and not a follower, and he impressed me with his ability to speak, make decisions, and set goals. A charismatic and humble person, he is a great friend.

Paul Hopkins was the fourth CEO in my career at Farmers Insurance Group. What a personality! A real go-getter and

decision maker, but also humble and charming. He is a true leader and a great friend.

Jeffrey and Ana Hastings

With 28-years of insurance experience, he knows what it takes to run a successful agency. He is passionate about helping others and is committed to their success. He became my district manager in 1998 and helped me develop systems in my business that are still being used today. He not only talked about running a better business, he was committed to helping others live their dreams and making a difference in this world.

Percy and Susana (Mune) Townsend are two of our closest friends. Percy has quite a personality. He is very organized, so much so that his life runs on a meticulous schedule. It works for him, and that's great. But when he is with me, he gets to cut loose and relax. I have learned many things from him over the years. He is a big fan of Colombian culture, and I really enjoy when we get together for any occasion. We always have something to talk about.

Mune knows the calendar better than anybody I know. If you ask her what day of the week the 21st of May is, she will tell you right away. She knows everybody's birthday, and she's always doing something or organizing an event or a get-together. She is a happy person who loves to dance – she even showed Percy how to dance a *mapale*, which is a typical Colombian dance. Everyone she meets loves her because of her personality and charisma.

Oswaldo and Alicia Puentes

Oswaldo is charismatic, upstanding and passionate about his family. All great qualities to have in a friend. I met him in 1973 at the University of Houston. We were in the same class, and everybody was introducing themselves by names and saying where they were from. He showed up late (as always, it turned out), so he introduced himself five minutes after I did. When he said he was from Colombia, people told him about me and, from that point forward, we became good friends. He has taught me many valuable lessons that I've carried with me throughout my life.

Germán and Mary Cortés

Germán is a wonderful person and a great friend. I met him and his family back in 1969, when I first came to Houston. He has been instrumental in guiding me and helping me become the person I am today. As for Mary, she is terrific, and she's the only person I know who can outlast everyone else at a party. She never gets tired!

John and Victoria Hughes

When I think of John, "watch out the English are coming" comes to mind. What an outstanding person! Among the many things we have in common, we are both ardent soccer fans. During the last World Cup in 2010, we saw every game played for 30 days, three to four games a day. That's the type of soccer fan we both are. I tell Victoria that she would be more financially secure if her last name were "Beckham" but I know she found the best man for her when she found John. I love you guys.

I have always been a motivated person. From the moment I was born, I knew I wanted to do something special with my life. I had dreams of becoming a famous musician and loved to listen to music. Growing up in Bogotá, Colombia I had always heard about how people lived in America and the freedom they had to work where they wanted to and become anyone they wanted to be. All they needed was the motivation to work hard and the passion to succeed. I had both and knew that if I had the opportunity, I could achieve everything. Little did I know that just a few years later, my opportunity to live in America was just around the corner. I would have a chance to live my dream and it would be up to me to make it a reality.

Writing this book was not easy. Having to put personal stories down of the hard times and mistakes you have made in your life are never easy to admit, much less right them down for the world to read. But the truth is if my story can help just one person get motivated enough to take action and improve their life, it is worth the embarrassment and the time.

As you will soon see, I wasn't born into money. The point is that if I can do something with my life, then so can you! With hard work and a few good ideas that you put into action, you can do anything you set out to do and live the American Dream. I wanted to deliver the message that life's experiences, if used and reflected on wisely, can help you build character and contribute to your personal development. One of the most important messages I have gleaned from my own life's experiences is that nothing replaces knowledge and learning. I first discovered that in high school at John Foster Dulles High School and then in college at the University of Houston-Downtown. To this day, I am still learning something from a broad range of sources, from the University of Farmers, where I can enhance my professional knowledge, to people that I meet every day. No matter the situation, there is always something to learn.

And finally, I personally wanted to thank the people who have shaped me and made me the person I am today. I know that I couldn't have done this alone. Through friendship and continued self-improvement I was able to meet my goals and develop a successful business that has given me the life I always dreamed of. Anyone can accomplish this simply by working on it day after day. It makes you a better person in every respect.

FOREWORD

For centuries, people have flocked to the United States with little more than a suitcase and the American Dream to be free. To immigrants who set out on the long and dangerous journey, often having to leave behind loved ones, "Freedom" is more than just a word. To some, freedom means being able to choose their own career path or way to worship. While to others, it means living a life without the fear of prosecution, poverty, famine, disease and in some cases - enslavement.

While we all may have our own definition of "freedom" or what the American Dream really means to us, the common thread to our beliefs and values lies somewhere in our innate desire to be happy. It is this search for happiness that keeps us going when times get tough; it is this search for happiness that gives us a reason to live.

Unfortunately, those of us who are born into abundance often live a life filled with expectations and feelings of entitlement. Instead of being happy and thankful for what we have, we end up complaining about little things that in the end really do not matter. Without true suffering we become an entire community of spoiled, stressed out people who fail to see how precious our time on earth really is until it is too late.

We have all heard the saying that while we cannot control everything that happens to us, we can control our reaction, and it is this reaction, which controls our attitude about life, love and happiness. Conditioning our mind in this manner to be thankful for our blessings takes conscious effort and does not come easy for most. However, for people like Gonzalo Jimenez and the millions of immigrants who travelled to our country for a better life, they understand and truly appreciate all of the luxuries we have been blessed with in our country today.

If you have not had the pleasure of getting to know him, Gonzalo is a man of passion and a love for life second to none. He lives each day to the fullest and loves music and all types of sports; but what he loves to do most is to make others laugh. Though his hard work, he has grown one of the most successful insurance agencies in the country. However if you ask Gonzalo about what he is most proud of, he does not define his success by the money he earns or by the things he has acquired; rather Gonzalo defines his success by the people's lives he has touched and the loving family that surrounds him each and every day.

When I hear someone talk about the American Dream, I think about Gonzalo Jimenez. Over the past 16 years, I have gotten to know him and his family on a very personal level. There are many stories I could tell you about what makes him stand out from others. I could tell you about his struggles he had to overcome growing up in Bogotá, Colombia as a young child. From the sudden and tragic loss of his sister to the difficult relationship he had with his father; Gonzalo maintains a positive attitude no matter what life throws his way.

I think about the night we were celebrating in a bar and watching the world cup when suddenly, for no apparent reason, Gonzalo stood up from his chair and gently placed his hand on his heart. Quietly, in the distance, I could hear the TV in the background playing the US National Anthem. I had always been told to stand up and do the same as a young child, but for some reason, I just stopped. As I sit there quietly but intently watching Gonzalo look at the American Flag waving in wind on the television, I could almost feel his emotion as he was reflecting on his life long journey to pursue the American Dream. It is this journey and appreciation for life, love and country that makes him the man he is today. I am excited that Gonzalo is sharing his experience with you and honored to be the one to write the Foreword to this amazing story.

Gonzalo, you have taught me through your hard work how to create a business that gives me a better life. You have taught me through your wisdom how to lead others. You have taught me through your words how to focus and how to be a caring and compassionate friend. You have taught me through your passion how to live life to the fullest. And finally, you have taught me through your love how to love, be loved and live each day with no regrets. You are indeed a role model for us all. Your faith is inspirational. Your hope is contagious and your love is unconditional. As is said in 1 Corinthians 13: "And now these three remain: faith, hope and love. But the greatest of these is love."

I love you dearly,

Jeff Hastings
Certified EMyth Business Coach
Houston, TX

EMyth

INTRODUCTION

My name is Gonzalo. I am the second of three children. I am a very humble person, and I take life one day at a time, but with one thing in mind: To always meet my short- and long-term goals. The most important thing that anybody can do is believe in one's own goals and abilities.

Most people get involved in business thinking, "If John Doe is successful in his business, I can be, too." But it's just not that easy, and it's important to think through every aspect of a business before launching one. First of all, you have to be very good administrator. You have to know how to manage your finances, and you have to have knowledge about the field or business you are getting into. The best way to do that is to learn the ins and outs of that particular business by working in it for couple of years.

As an entrepreneurial person, I give people the opportunity to work in my company and not only develop themselves as human beings, but also to grow with my company. Those are the types of opportunities I received over the years from different employers, and I am very grateful to them. My hobbies are music (I have a huge collection), song writing, abstract art painting, traveling, soccer (attended 1998 world cup soccer in France) and football (I follow every season -- "Go Texans").

Since I was young, the motivational part of me has provided me the incentive to take action in anything I confront in life. This spirit and passion prompted me to write this story about my life. I hope you enjoy reading it and will be inspired to take action in your own life.

CHAPTER ONE

Humble Beginnings

"You have to love yourself first, in order to love the ones around you."
Gonzalo Jimenez

I was born in Bogotá, Colombia on October 10, 1952. That day, I had the first accident of my life; after delivering me, the pediatrician accidentally dropped some kind of acid in my right eye, which partially burned my eye and hurt my cornea. The result was that I became cross-eyed and lost nearly 90 percent of the sight in my right eye.

My parents put me in physical therapy for many years, in an attempt to correct the condition to restore my sight. In 1953, they brought me to a medical center in New York to start a new therapy that they believe might help me. We spent three months at a time at the center and, after the initial treatments, we returned every two years until I was about eight years old. Every time I went for therapy, I spent three months in New York. By the time I turned eight, my left eye was in position back again, but my right eye still suffered from dramatic sight loss.

Despite this precarious beginning, I was a very happy child growing up. As far back as I can remember, I had everything a child could ask for, as did my sister, María Yolanda, who was two years older, and my brother Dwight, who was four years younger. We all had lots of good times and good memories. I remember how much I loved music, ever since I was just a toddler. In fact, one Christmas my parents gave me an accordion that was taller than I was. From then on, when my family had a get-together, they always ask me to play it. Since then, I play melodies by ear.

My father use to take us to a small town called Gualanday that was about three hours outside the capital city of Bogotá. This town had then – and still has – the most beautiful views of the river going across town. It was, and still is, one of the things that I enjoy the most. In fact, my father went to Gualanday so often that people there called him to be the godfather of many children.

The second thing I remember the most vividly is that my father was into horseracing. My father had two fillies, one named *La Cumparcita* and the other was *Veronica*. La Cumparcita was always first out of the gate and managed to stay ahead of the pack by 10 or 20 lengths until the end of the race, when she inevitably fell behind to lose. As for Veronica, she was also fast as a bullet, but she had more stamina. This horse went on to win about 15 races, and had several second and third place showings. I cannot put words to the joy and emotions this filly gave us for so many years. Every time *Veronica* won a race, the entire family would get together for a post-victory celebration. Then one day in one of her races, she fell in the starting gate, broke her neck and ultimately had to be put down.

We had a lot of fun going to the racetrack every Saturday to watch the horses train and on Sundays to see them race. It was at the racetrack that my father taught us how to gamble for fun, not for money. Every Sunday, he would give us 20 pesos to use and bet with for the whole day. Tickets cost two pesos each, so he always told us that if we wanted to spend the entire 20 pesos on one race that was fine. However, if we lost it, he would not give us a penny more that day.

This was my father's way of teaching us how to manage money. Here is how he started: Instead of giving us allowances for school, he gave us five pesos per week to spend any way we chose. Most of the other kids we knew were carrying around two or three pesos per day. At the time, I questioned my father, but as I matured, I began to appreciate the way in which he guided us and showed us how to manage our money. I think that some of my success in the business world is thanks to the early lessons my father taught me.

When I was in middle school, I enjoyed playing sports, especially soccer and basketball. In addition to sports, I sang in the school chorus. Every Thursday at noon, we went to my father's parents' house for lunch. It was a special treat that I looked forward to every week. Easter Week was also a great tradition. On Good Friday, the whole family got together for lunch every year in the same house. The main dish was sardines with rice and a few other ingredients. We would eat and then, because it was Good Friday, we would spend all afternoon listening to the radio, to a program called "Las Siete Palabras," (The Seven Words) a referral to the last seven sentences spoken by Christ when he was on the cross.

CHAPTER TWO

Home Life in Bogotá, Colombia

"There is scarcely any passion without struggle."
Albert Camus

One day, we noticed things beginning to change in our home. We realized that my father and mother were having marital problems. At the time, I was about 11 years old but I noticed how things were different. My father would show up late at night and argue constantly with my mother, or she would get angry with him and provoke an argument. That went on for quite some time until we finally knew the family love was diminished and the family harmony gone. The only thing that mattered was to provide for all the financial needs of the three children: my sister, my brother and me.

My parents were actually more concerned about their own personal goals and problems than those of their children were. Of course, they were always there to support us financially and help us with homework or anything else related to excelling in our studies, but for them affection was a secondary notion. For example, when I was 12 years old, my parents ordered me to accompany my 14-year-old sister to parties. She had invitations coming in, but in order for her to go to any of those parties; I had to go with her as a sort of chaperone. In my parents' way of thinking, I was along to protect my sister. What they did not know was that I was so shy; she had to bribe me most of the time with chocolates or candies. That went on for a couple of years.

By the time I was 14, my sister, who was 16 at the time, was suffering from constant headaches. My parents took her to different doctors and specialists; nobody could diagnose what was causing the headaches. They even took her to one of the most prominent eye doctors in Colombia, who simply pronounced that she was pushing her eyes too hard, and that was causing the headaches. He prescribed glasses, and the headaches continued. Then, things got worse.

One day in December 1966, we were out of town and suddenly my sister was stricken with a terrible headache; she started rolling her eyes and shaking. My parents immediately took her to a hospital in Bogotá. As soon as we arrived, she was whisked into the emergency room and then intensive care, where she lasted just a few hours. María Yolanda passed away the next day, leaving us with a deep sorrow. It took me about 15 years to stop crying every time that I thought about her. The day after she died, my sister was taken to church and then to the cemetery. I cried so much for so long that, even today, my eyes get watery just thinking about it. My father, who used to smoke cigarettes, stopped for good that day.

If things were not bad enough with the death of my sister, they proceeded to get worse. A year after that tragic event, my father had an affair with another woman. It turned into a relationship and, out of their relationship came a child, a son named Gonzalo Alberto. In the years that followed, I would ask my father why in the world he called his other son by my exact name, but he never had an answer for me. The situation with my mother fell apart when she found out about the affair. As I said before, their adult problems were the priority, and we kids were often an afterthought.

At that time, I started rebelling and doing stupid or crazy things -- nothing to be ashamed of and nothing dangerous, but things I regret to this day. For instance, I sold some precious silver items that belonged to my parents so I could have extra money to do things I wanted to do. One time, my cousin, Germán, and I planned an entire weekend away and tricked our parents into thinking we were spending the weekend at the other's house. Instead, we went to a city called Girardot. On arriving, we asked my father's cousin, Gustavo, if we could stay with him for the weekend. At first, he agreed, but the next morning he contacted my parents, discovered our lie, and put us back on the first bus to Bogotá.

I have plenty of school stories to tell, but that is not the point of this book. I would however, like to recall one particular story that happened during my 10th-grade year. I had two close friends in my class; people called us The Three Musketeers because we did everything together, even getting into trouble. In one particular class, we had devised a way to use cheat sheets during tests, and we always all had the same grade as a result. Therefore, the teacher, Mr. Vargas, told us one day that we would not be allowed to sit together. That were around 40 students in that class, so he really had to do some creative reshuffling. He put me in the back right-hand corner of the classroom; Ordoñez, one of my friends, was sent to the back left-hand side of the classroom; and Rodriguez, the third friend, was assigned a front-row seat. Mr. Vargas told us that he would see just how smart we really were the next time he gave a test. We knew we had to create something new...but what?

During the next test, we took our seats across the room from each other, as Mr. Vargas prepared to walk the whole class back and forward during the entire period. The test began, and I used the cheat sheets I had to answer the test while he was walking back and forth checking for potential cheaters. When I finished, I used tape to stick the cheat sheets on Mr. Vargas' coattail when he walked past my desk. When he walked past my friend's desk, my friend took the cheat sheets, copied them down and then placed them back on the coattails for the third of the Musketeers to copy. We continued to do well in that class – we even had the same grades – and he never found out how we were doing it.

I am not proud of what I did. Truthfully, I am glad those days are gone and that I am mature enough now to make smart decisions. What I have come to realize is that, after parents, teachers are the ones who guide us and help motivate us to be somebody in our future. For all their hard work, they are underpaid, mistreated by the system and students, and nobody does anything to change it. My brother in law's wife, Zulema Garcia, was a teacher. Despite the low salary she received, she spent her own money on classroom supplies the school did not have. These are the actions of a good person full of heart, like many of our teachers.

In those days, I also felt that I had to be a guide for my brother Dwight. I tried to play the role of father, guiding him in the decisions he made, until I realized that I was playing that role out of anger. I was angry with my parents for not giving us the love, understanding, and compassion that every child needs and should receive. Fortunately, as I pointed out before, they provided us with financial security, education and a roof over our heads. One of the things that I cannot forgive my father for was his inability to be the grandfather I wanted and expected him to be. From the moment my wife and I had our first child, my father behaved like the stock market, many up and downs but not much affection to spare for my children.

One event, in particular, really opened my eyes. On Christmas Eve 1980, my wife and I took our two boys, Jason and Bryan, to my father's home to deliver a Christmas present. When we arrived, there was another person with him, so we said hello and my oldest son walked over to my father to present the gift. My father took it and completely ignored his grandson. When I saw what he had done – or had not done – that was it for me. I told my wife that we should leave before I did something stupid. We told my father to have a very nice Christmas with his friend, and we left. It would be another four years before I saw my father again.

My relationship with my father was fraught with stress and strife over the years. We had high points and low points, and we often went for long periods without speaking. One day, for example, he called me at the office and asked if he could drop by. He said that he owed me an apology that he was sorry for the person he had been in the past and he wanted to apologize in person. So I agreed. In addition, when he showed up, I told him I would be happy for a reconciliation, but I also wanted him to apologize to my wife, which he did. The problem was – and continued to be – that he was always apologizing for his behavior, so after a couple of years, I cut off communication once again.

Then one day, when my family and I were already living in Houston, he called me from Colombia. Once again, he wanted to apologize. He also told me that he was living with another woman, not my mother, and he asked me if they (he and his girlfriend) could move in with us for about a month until they could be settled and find an apartment. I told him that I would confer with Luz and get back to him. Generous and noble person that she is, my wife said, "Of course he can come; he's your dad." By then, we had three children, and we moved one out of his bedroom to accommodate my father and his girlfriend.

About three weeks later, my father showed up, with not only his girlfriend but also his girlfriend's mother. That was quite a surprise. Even so, we decided to handle it as politely as possible. Moreover, that is exactly what we did until nearly three weeks into their stay in our house, when I realized I had not seen him looking for an apartment or making any effort to find a place to live. When I asked him about his plans to move out, his response was, "Are we causing you any problems?" They were not, but I said he had to look for and find apartment soon. My children were living very uncomfortably, and he had promised they would be with us for 30 days. Things went badly after that. He retreated to their room, and they proceeded to use it as a bunker. They only emerged to go to the bathroom, and they join us for any meals or take any food from the kitchen.

A couple of days after that encounter, I came home from work to find his girlfriend in the living room. I asked her to speak to my father and make him see reason. Her response was, "He is your father. Fix your own problems." That was the last straw for me. I completely lost my temper and told her that they had five days to get out of my house. What we did not know was that the day after I ordered them out of the house, my father invented a story about my wife teaching our daughter to say that my father's girlfriend was our maid. In Spanish, the word *sirvienta* means "servant" and is considered demeaning. He was clearly trying to create rifts in my family, and that made me even angrier. My father knew that I would never speak to anyone like that, much less teach my children to. When I found out what he had attempted to do, I told him that he had to leave in four days. I could not understand how he could hurt us so much and show so little respect for my children. He brought only sorrow to my family.

Unfortunately, that was not the worst of it. In late May 2012, Luz and I were invited to an event that our son, Jason, was attending. It was a seminar designed for participants to explore and discover their strengths and weaknesses, and how they could harness their strengths to get ahead in life. When we arrived, Jason was talking to the people he invited, including my wife, my other son and his wife, my daughter, his own wife and three other people. He told each of them what it meant to him that they were at the seminar and how each of them played an important role in helping him become the person he was. He thanked everyone, that is, except me. "What I have to say about you will be said in front of everyone later," he said, smiling sadly.

The featured speaker explained what the program was all about and then introduced those participants who were willing to share their experiences with the program with the audience. There were six who went up on stage; my son was one of them. When his turn came, he talked about the impact the program had on him and how it helped him find himself. Then he shocked me by mentioning the episode in which I gave my father five days to get out of our house. In Jason's mind, I was wrong. I insulted my own father and I was disrespectful. That experience, Jason said, stuck with him so much so that he built a wall between us, not just me but also his mother.

For years leading up to that night, Luz and I had asked ourselves what we did wrong, what we did for him to be so reserved with us but not anybody else. Why didn't he want to spend time in our house and with his family? Thanks to this program, he found himself and gained enough courage to ask me to forgive him for not allowing me to be the father I wanted to be all those years. What a moment it was! Everyone applauded. My wife and I started crying for joy; we had our son back.

My father moved back to Colombia and started having health issues two years later. His caregiver called one day to let me know that my father was very ill. Despite our rocky history, I went to Bogotá with my wife, my brother, and his wife, to visit. We took him to the doctor and got the best medical attention available. He improved a little, but he knew his health was deteriorating because he asked us all for our forgiveness then. After a 10-day visit, we came back to Houston. Three months later, he became very ill with pneumonia and passed away. We all went to Bogotá for his funeral. While it was a sad occasion, I remembered that my father left us at peace with himself. We had reconciled, and that was what really mattered.

CHAPTER THREE

My First Love

"A true man does not need to romance a different girl every night...
a true man romances the same girl for the rest of her life."
Ana Alas

My last name on my father's side is Jimenéz; I get my strength and my independence from that side of the family. My mother's family name is Bernal, and from them I inherited a happy nature, a love of music and a sense of humor; I love telling and hearing jokes. I am also related to one of the past presidents of Colombia, Miguel Abadia Méndez, who was my mother's great-grandfather. He was Colombia's president from 1926 to 1930. This combination of strength and humor, independence and leadership has enabled me to deal with adversity, to always meet the goals that I set for myself and to accomplish anything I put my mind to.

Strength and a positive outlook are important qualities to have in matters of the heart. I had my first romantic relationship when I was 15. My first girlfriend was Esperanza. It was a very beautiful and pure relationship, and I cared for her very much. But we were young and immature, and we wound up in going and growing in different directions. She eventually married, had three children and moved to Los Angeles. In late December 2010, my mother called to tell me that Esperanza had thrown herself in front of a train and committed suicide. It later came out that she had struggled with depression since her mother's death from cancer. Incredibly, at the time, her father also had cancer, as did one of her daughters.

Sadly, for Esperanza, the burden was too heavy. After Esperanza and I ended our relationship and went our separate ways, I met Patricia at a party hosted by one of my cousins. She lived across the street from him in a subdivision called Primero de Mayo. We enjoyed each other's company; we both liked to dance and have fun. There were plenty of good times for a while, until she moved to New York City to live with her sister Constanza. Then, in late 1968, my mother's family threw a party and introduced to me Gloria Esperanza, the daughter of my mother's cousin. I liked her so much that I asked her out right away, and just days after our first date, we were an item. For six months, we were together constantly, enjoying each other's company.

In mid-1969, however, I moved to Houston, Texas for school, while she stayed in Bogotá finishing her college studies. For the next four years, we kept our relationship going. We spoke on the phone twice a week every week; I went to Bogotá every year to visit her for a month at a time. Everything seemed fine and on track until one day, I received a phone call from my brother-in-law, who told me that she was going out with someone else. I could not believe it. I did not want to believe it. But I had to take him seriously because why would he lie? I decided to travel to Colombia to surprise her, and I didn't tell anybody I was coming.

I arrived on a Friday, and by 6:00 pm, I was knocking on her front door. When she saw me, she almost fainted. She kissed me and hugged me, and I asked her to invite me in, which she did. Sure enough, the new person in her life was standing in her dining room. She introduced him as a friend, but I knew better. Apparently he knew me. He did not wait long, five minutes maybe, before excusing himself and leaving. Gloria Esperanza did not know what to do, so she ran upstairs, crying like crazy, and locked herself in her bedroom.

Her mother came down to see what happened, saw me and greeted me as always, with courtesy and warmth. I was sure she felt badly about what her daughter had done to me. I went to Gloria Esperanza's room to ask her what had happened, what had changed for her. She opened the door and apologized, but said she did not know how to fix the unfixable. For me, that was the beginning of the end. Even if she had wanted me back, I could not forgive her.

The timing could not have been better. Three months after I walked away from Gloria Esperanza, I won the jackpot, the mega million lottery, when I met a woman named Luz Marina. Funny how the best things in life happen. I was with a friend of mine the day I met her, and we were bored. So he started calling old girlfriends, but they were all busy. Then he called his actual girlfriend, Noemi, asked her out, and told her to invite another girl to come dancing with us because I needed someone to dance with. As it turned out, Noemi invited my future wife.

We had a great time at the disco that night. We spent all night dancing and talking – I could not believe how much I liked her. At the end of the evening, I asked her for a kiss, to which she replied, "You don't have to ask." From that day in September 1976, we started dating. It was a whirlwind courtship. I loved her romantically and as a friend and companion. We spent hours together doing things, we loved to do; I would drive miles to be with her. That lasted three months, until we married on December 3, 1976.

Since day one, our marriage has been an adventure. On our wedding day, I tried to get a taxi to get to the church, and every taxi that drove by was occupied. Since I was running late, I decided to get on a bus just to get there. People were staring at me since I was dressed up in a traditional wedding costume. Fortunately, I got there just in time. The bride, it turned out, was also running late. We waited for her for at least 15 minutes. What we did not know was that my cousin was driving her to the church in my car and the battery had a loose cable. The car would not start at first, but finally he got it going and arrived late at church. We were married and then had a beautiful reception in my Uncle Alfonso's house.

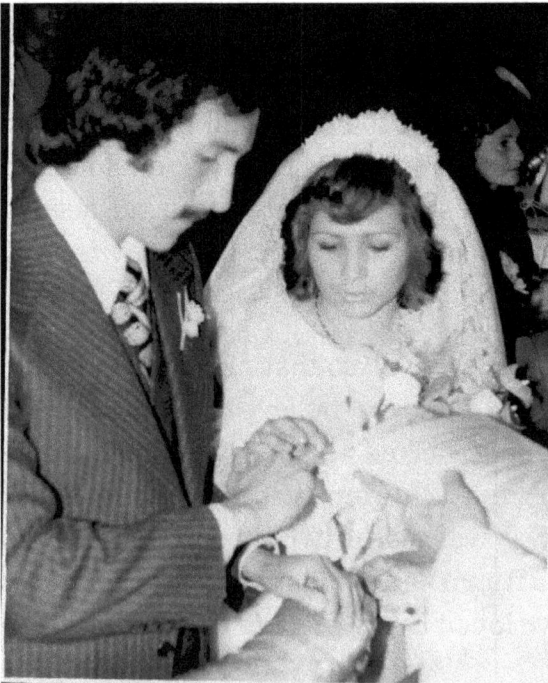

By one o'clock in the morning, we were ready to leave for our honeymoon destination, which was a three-hour drive from Bogotá. We waved goodbye to everyone and took off. Two hours later, we heard an explosion; I stopped, thinking it was a flat tire. I asked my new wife to check and see, but she could not find anything wrong with the tires. So we opened the trunk and found that one of the champagne bottles had uncorked and exploded all over the trunk. There was champagne everywhere. Once we finally we got to our destination, the honeymoon began; I was 26 years old, and she was 24.

Looking back now, I realize that when we married that day. I loved Luz very much. But I don't think I was *in love* until about two years later following a series of events caused by my own immaturity. I learned something the hard way. Once I was married, I kept thinking about my old relationship with Gloria Esperanza. I couldn't stop thinking about her and why she did what she did. So I got in touch with her again and asked her to go out with me, which she did many times. When I did ask her out, I would show up only two out of three, and when I did show up I was cold, although sometimes I was angry. I have to admit that I was bitter and resentful, not because I was still in love with her but because I wanted to get back at her for all the pain she had caused me. This went on for quite some time, although in my mind I didn't think I was harming anybody. I was wrong, immature and selfish. I was thinking only about myself, not my wife or my son, who was born on September 26, 1977.

Between the time that I had gotten married and the birth of my son, I was busy destroying my marriage with my selfishness and thoughtlessness. Because of my behavior, my marriage was on the verge of collapse. Then one day, while my brother and his family were visiting us from Houston, my wife overheard me make a comment to my brother about the relationship I was having with my old girlfriend. And she reacted the way anybody would, with hurt and disappointment. I was not, it seemed, the man she had thought I was.

Right after that, I left the house in order to avoid further hurting her, and once again I was wrong. I should have stayed and comforted her, as she deserved, which I did the following day after I came back. But the damage was already done. Fortunately, she stuck with me, and I consider myself a lucky man to have found such a sweet, noble and lovely woman to share my life with. I am grateful that she is the woman she is.

I am doubly grateful when I remember how badly my parents treated her during the first years of our marriage. For reasons only they knew, my parents did not accept my wife when we were married and for several years afterwards. In fact, my mother mistreated her for the first four years of our marriage until we moved back to the U.S. with our sons in 1980. The worst of it was that I allowed it to happen and to continue because she was my mother. Now, with the benefit of hindsight and age, I regret allowing my mother to treat my wife the way she did and speak to her the way she did. Still, things can change – and they did. Years later, when my wife and I brought my mother from Colombia, she was a different person with a different attitude. She suddenly began treating Luz with the respect she deserved. As a result, the relationship did an about-face in a very positive way. Now, she sees my wife as the daughter she lost 45 years ago.

In 1983, Luz and I bought our first house. We made many beautiful memories in that house, raising children and hosting family celebrations. Despite the ballooning mortgage payments and interest rates, despite the high cost of living in that house, we all loved it. It was a family house. Speaking of family, my wife and I have three children. Jason, my oldest, was born on September 26, 1977 in Bogotá. Of my three kids, he has always been the respectful one, the organizer and the goal-setter. As a young boy, he loved sports. He played football, baseball, and soccer, and was on the All-Star teams in both baseball and football. Jason graduated from Kempner High School and went to the University of Houston intending to study business, but wound up putting his career on hold when he became interested in my business: insurance. He took a break from school to work at my insurance agency for a couple of years, and then went on to become an insurance agent himself, opening his own agency in 1999. His success speaks for itself, as he is one of the biggest assets Farmers has. He has also been very successful in his personal life; he and his lovely wife, Jessica, have two beautiful children, Vianni Juliana and Nicolás.

My second child, Bryan, was also born in Bogotá, but a few years later on January 29, 1980. More temperamental than his older brother, Bryan was also an All-Star athlete from a young age. When he turned 15, however, he discovered his love of cars, how to drive them and how to drive them very fast. So he began networking and getting to know those people who could help him in his ambition to become one of the greatest drivers in drag racing. He accomplished that with honors, participating in races around the country and winning many different awards. He also attended the University of Houston for a while, until he opened his own mechanic shop to work on his beloved cars. Now, he runs my office along with his sister, Gina Lee, and has been doing it with great success. Bryan has three children: my oldest granddaughter, Karina Nicole, from his first marriage, and then Gianna Vanessa and Bryan Anthony from his second marriage to the lovely Jennifer.

My youngest one, Gina Lee, was born in the U.S. She is a native Texan, born on April 27, 1984 in Houston. She has always been her own person, caring, sweet and very active. When she was younger, she played softball and volleyball, and she was a cheerleader. But she was not as devoted to sports as her brothers were. She studied business administration at University of Texas, and graduated in the summer of 2009. Not long afterward, she married Ignacio Garza, and they now have two gorgeous girls, my granddaughters Camilla Sophia and Samantha Lee.

There is nothing like having kids, and when they have children – our grandchildren – it makes everything that much more special. Looking at my grandchildren and seeing my own children in their facial expressions and the way they move makes me remember the wonderful moments I've shared with my children over the years. One of the greatest experiences I ever had with Jason and Bryan was when we went to the World Cup soccer tournament in France in 1998. We traveled to Paris, Montpellier, and some other cities following the Colombian soccer team for almost three weeks. In between our travel days, we saw most of the games in the greatest atmosphere of joy in the world. There is nothing quite like soccer to unite millions of people. I feel very fortunate that my kids and I were able to share that incredible adventure.

Bryan Jimenez, his wife Jennifer, and children Karina, Gianna & Bryan

menez, his wife Jessica, and children Vianni and Nicolas

Gina Jimenez Garza and husband Nacho Garza (above); daughters Camilla and Sammy (below)

My in-laws, I love you guys

One thing I will never forget was the day Luz and I renewed our vows in December 2001, in niversary. We did it ass in Las Vegas. est friends were with e renewed our vows ers, then went for taurant inside the ntastic day. I felt like how special Luz it I was. Our children aid of honor. What a moment—it was truly memorable.

CHAPTER FOUR

My School Years

"Failure in anything that you pursue is the first step to conquer success."
Gonzalo Jimenez

I was not the best student, but I was smart enough to conquer most things that came my way. In Colombia, I attended a Catholic school for 11 years. As for my behavior, I was the Dennis the Menace of my class, kind of wild and crazy. But I always had respectable grades because I very good at remembering what was taught in class, which mean that I didn't really study for quizzes or tests or exams. My success continued over the years until one day, on the first day of 11th grade, the physics teacher said my name during attendance and asked me to leave the classroom. When I asked why, he told me that I had to leave because of my bad behavior the previous year. So I left the room for that period.

I kept leaving the classroom during that period for the next two months until one day I realized that if or when my father found out about this, he was not going to like it. And he would be especially angry to see a zero on my report card. Therefore, I opted to go back to class and see what happened. It was a turnaround moment in my life. When I went back for the first time and sat down at my desk, the teacher told me in front of 40 students to get out of his class. But I refused. "I'm here to learn, not to do as you command," I said. He threatened to physically remove me himself, but I would not budge. I told him that I had as much right to learn as anybody else.

Then he lost his temper and came after me, but I grabbed the empty desk in front me mine and held it in front of me like a shield. When I did that, he hit the desk instead of me and then announced he was going to the principal's office. When he and the principal returned, I was waiting outside the classroom. I figured enough drama had happened for one day. The principal took me back to his office, but did not allow me to explain what had happened. Instead, he expelled me and ordered me to bring my parents to his office right away. So I went home to talk to my father and explain the whole situation, but he insisted that we go back to school.

Once there, my father went directly to the teacher's class and asked him to come out and speak with us. The first thing my father asked was why I'd been barred from class since the beginning of the year and then why nobody from the school had reported that action to me. It came out that the teacher had not only thrown me out of class based on another teacher's report from the previous year, but he had also never reported it to the administration. My father was furious. So we went to the principal's office, and again my father asked the same questions. However, the principal would not budge; the decision to expel me was final.

At that moment, I felt that my life was about to change for good. And it did. Eight days after this incident, I decided to ask my parents for help in starting a new life in Houston, Texas. As it happened, my aunt lived there at that time, so I thought that, with a little help from my parents and my aunt, I would be in good shape to start over. So I asked them for permission to take my brother, Dwight, with me to continue our studies. At the time, I was 17 and he was 13. My plan was to first find an efficiency we could live in, and then we would register for whichever school was in my aunt's neighborhood. The only snag was that my aunt lived in the suburbs, and that meant we would need a car. Thankfully, my parents were kind enough to buy one for us.

I called my aunt and made sure our plan met with her approval, which it did. What I did not know was that since Dwight and I were younger than 18, our aunt needed to have guardianship rights in order for us to get student visas from the American embassy. She and her husband agreed to it, and I have been grateful ever since. After a month of waiting for the guardianship papers to arrive, we finally got them and went straight to the embassy, where they issued our student visas. It was one of the happiest days of my life; it felt as if my dreams were finally underway and life was really beginning. A few weeks later, we were on our way to the land of opportunity.

We traveled with my parents from Bogotá to Miami, and from there we rented a car and drove to Houston. I remembered that my aunt told us that she lived about a mile from a K-Mart store, so when we entered the Houston city limits and I saw a K-Mart sign, I was sure we were near her home. What we did not know was that there were more than 30 stores around Houston, and this particular store was nearly 30 miles from her home. We called my aunt to ask her how to get to her house and when we told her where we were, we realized that it was about 30 K-Marts around Houston and we were about 30 miles from her house. When we arrived, we sat up late talking for hours.

The next morning we got up early to register at John Foster Dulles High School in Stafford, Texas. Since we were arriving in the middle of the school year, the registrar told us that we would start school right away, the next day, in fact, so my father took us out that very day and bought us a car. The plan was to stay in my aunt's house as little time possible and then live with my brother in our own apartment somewhere in or near central Houston. My father provided us with three months' rent and a car, but after that, I would have to pay rent and survive.

And that's exactly what we did. My father stayed for about a week and then went home, but my mother stayed with us in my aunt's house for another month while we found an apartment and moved in. After she returned to Bogotá, I started looking for a job. I found one in a candle factory, where I worked the late shift from four o'clock in the afternoon until midnight for about a year. When I saw that the late hours were affecting my schoolwork, I took a different job, this time in a restaurant where my oldest cousin, Alex, worked. In addition, my brother and I went to work for the Houston Chronicle delivering the daily newspaper in the wee hours of the morning. So I delivered papers, went to school and then went to work in the restaurant. That was my life and my routine until I graduated in 1972.

My senior year in high school, I realized that, in order to keep my student visa current, I had to keep continue my studies after graduation. I wanted desperately to stay, so I went to the University of Houston to register for some basic courses to comply with the visa requirements. It was not as easy as I thought it would be. As an international student, my fees were almost double those of a resident or citizen, and I did not have that kind of money. It all came to a head when my mother came to visit. Her tourist visa was about to expire, so I took her to an immigration office to ask for a two-month extension. While I was in the waiting room, she went to speak with an immigration officer, who asked her the usual questions of why she was there and who she was visiting.

The officer then called me in and asked me what I was doing in Houston, and I told him that I was about to graduate from high school. When he followed up by asking me if I was registered to attend a college or university after graduation, I answered him honestly: that I was not because I didn't have the money. His response was, "Mr. Jiménez, you have 15 days to leave the country, and when you have the money to register you will be welcome back to United States."

That day, I returned to my apartment with no visa extension for my mother and the threat of having to leave hanging over my head. I had to come up with a Plan B to stay in the U.S. legally, but I had final exams the following week at school and the state standardized test in just a few days. That is when I had the bright idea of failing the government test so I couldn't graduate and would have to stay in school one more year. At least it would be one more year of saving money for college. The day of the test came, and I purposely answered 90 percent of the questions incorrectly. What I did not know was my high GPA in school was enough to qualify me for a cap and gown; I didn't need to ace the government test. So much for Plan B.

Graduation day came, and I walked up to receive my diploma by myself. My parents were not there to see it, and my only satisfaction was that I had accomplished this on my own. A few days later, I was on my way back to Colombia, without a plan for getting back to the U.S. but with the will to figure something out quickly. From the minute I arrived back at my parents' house, I began thinking and planning how to get the money to go back. Nothing was going to stop me from going to college. Two weeks into my stay, I was visiting my uncle and his wife, Olga, and telling them about my situation, when a solution presented itself. Or should I say that Olga became my guardian angel. She offered to lend me $3,000 to go to college. "Gonzalo, I know that when you want something you get it so I am going to lend you the money that you need for you to reach your goal," she said. "Pay me back whenever you can."

That was that. One week later, I was back in the U.S., registering for classes at the University of Houston and thinking I would get a degree in data processing. When I was done there, I went back to my old job and asked the manager if he would rehire me. He did not hesitate. And he offered me a great piece of advice: "Always leave the doors open in any previous job because you never know when you might need it again." I was back on the job three days after landing in Houston.

At my very first class, the professor asked everybody to introduce themselves. As we went around the room, I heard a person say, "I am Oswaldo Puentes from Colombia, South America." I could not believe it. When class was over, I introduced myself and we started talking. He told me that he was living with his brother and sister-in-law; it was a stressful set-up because he did not have enough privacy or independence. So I asked if he wanted to share an apartment with my brother and me. A couple of days later he moved in with us, and a week after that he was working with us in the same restaurant.

Oswaldo became and still is a great friend. When I went with him to his brother's house to pick up his belongings, he asked me how in the world was it that I could afford a brand-new car on a busboy's wages. Here is what I told him: "That's the beauty of this country. As long as you have a job and good credit, you can have anything you want."

CHAPTER FIVE

Starting My Insurance Agency

"We can always live on less when we have more to live for."
S. Stephen McKenney

I lived in Bogotá on and off for four years, from 1976 to 1980, managing my father's company, Mediequipo Ltda. It was a medical equipment importer and exclusive distributor in Colombia for a U.S. company called Hycel. For those four years, I did very well selling and servicing medical equipment. But in October 1980, Luz and I decided to start over; we moved to Houston with our boys, who were then three years old and almost a year old at the time. I may have only had $1,500 in my pocket, but I had plenty of ambition.

Thanks to the generosity of my brother and sister-in-law, we had a place to stay while we looked for work and a place to live. It wasn't long before I found a job at a restaurant in the Galleria area. A few days after that, we rented an apartment and moved in. In order to make ends meet, Luz took a job in the housekeeping department of a Hilton hotel for a short time. However, with Luz working we had to resolve the issue of childcare. Daycare seemed to be the only option, but it was too expensive. We would be working just to pay for it. Luz suggested that we ask my mother if she would be willing to come to Houston to take care of our babies. Of course, she said 'yes,' and we began the legal process of bringing her to the U.S. to live with us.

A couple of months into our new life, I got a job at a company called Bowen Tools, which was in the business of manufacturing pipes for the oil industry. My job was to clean up the mess left by the machinists, and my shift ran from three o'clock in the afternoon until eleven o'clock at night. Then I would go home to sleep for a couple of hours, get up and shower, and deliver the Houston Chronicle, just like the good old days when I was in high school. It was a rough schedule but we made it work. In early 1981, my mother, who was divorced from my father by then, arrived to live with us.

Then in March 1981, I met a person in the apartment complex we lived in. His name was Manuel Montano, and he referred me for a job at a property management company that managed various apartment complexes I worked for them until July, when applied for a position with Fluor Ocean Services, an oil company. I worked there for nearly a year. In June 1982, I took the plunge and started my own business, Gonzalo Jimenez Insurance Agency, Inc.

I remember my wife asking me how in the world we were going to manage this change. We would have to cut some expenses, I told her, and live from her paycheck until my business was making money and I was getting commissions. A month went by, and my first commission check arrived, in the amount of $60. Compared to the $1,500 a month I made at Fluor, it was peanuts, but I asked Luz to be patient. I knew things would improve with time. Sure enough, every month after that the check got bigger and bigger.

During that first year, I ran the agency largely by myself, working on my own with my wife coming in to help out at the office on occasion. She even referred new clients, former colleagues at one of the companies she had worked for. After two years, my work plate was so full that I asked Luz to come and help me after work every day, which she did. I was grateful for her help, but I was also used to doing things a certain way in my office. Not surprisingly, we butted heads; she wanted to run the office her way, and I want it to run it mine. In the end, I broke down and hired a secretary for the sake of our marriage.

As time went on, the business keep growing and growing, so much so that I told Luz I really needed her help and guiding hand in the office more than ever. She agreed to come back on one condition: she would be in charge of operations and management, and I would run everything else. We both agreed that compromise was a good thing, and the situation improved tremendously. We were building a business with hard work and sacrifice, we had three children, and we had family willing to help so that we could fulfill our dreams. It was a glorious time.

There are 16,000 Farmers Insurance agencies around the country, and I'm proud to say that my agency is among the top one percent. I have no doubt that it's due to my 25 years of hard work and dedication. I became an agent and entrepreneur because I wanted to live the American dream. I got involved in the insurance initially based on a recommendation from my cousin Alejandro. He was representing Farmers Insurance at the time, and he suggested that I look for a district manager to get started. Steve Blakesley, who was district manager at the time, contracted me to join the program in June 1982, and my journey in entrepreneurialism began.

I vividly remember having to meet sales quotas in order to stay in the program. That was no easy task, considering that I didn't know the insurance business. Worse yet, I had no mentor, no guidance in how to do anything except fill out applications. I learned the hard way, by trial and error and through fellow agents who steered me in the right direction and showed me the ropes. One of the most important things I learned from them was the importance of building relationships. Once I was on the right business course, I began visiting realtors, mortgage companies, title companies and loan officers, mining those relationships for new business. Those efforts brought reward, as we began signing nearly all of our new clients through home sales. My system was to call every one of our customers when it was time to renew their policy, invite them to review their coverage, and then explain what their policy did and did not cover. If they were happy with our service, we would ask them to please refer our agency family members or friends. And that's how I built up my business. A satisfied client is the best advertising, and I am grateful to my clientele for all their support over the years. In 1998, Steve Blakesley, my first district manager, retired and was replaced by Jeffrey Hastings, who has turned out to be one of the best people I've ever met.

It is interesting how my evolution as an entrepreneur has made me what I am today. What I have learned is that it's important to go through the process or working one's way up – working in restaurants, delivering newspapers, cleaning houses and buildings – to understand the value of life's opportunities. If I had started as a coat-and-tie manager without ever having gotten my hands dirty, I would not understand what it means to start at the bottom and work my way up. Knowing what it is like to begin at the beginning has made my success in business that much sweeter. Now that my family and I are American citizens, I ask myself on occasion why some people born and raised in this country do not have the will to make sacrifices to pursue their dream. Having had the good fortune to born here; I can only assume they have not had to struggle to get ahead.

CHAPTER SIX

Attitude Makes All the Difference

"There are exactly as many special occasions in life as we choose to celebrate."
Robert Brault

This chapter is dedicated to focus, to a positive attitude and to passion in anything that we pursue in life.

Attitude is the most important part in any decision one makes. It is so important that when one acts with doubt or a negative attitude, the results are negative as well. Attitude is a critical component of the formula for success, the other part being passion. When combined, the results are fantastic. I think it is all in the way one thinks about and approaches situations. For instance, I look at all my problems as challenges, not obstacles. And when I think or plan anything, I set a date; otherwise, I only end up having thought about it, but not having done it.

Many people have been saying lately that the American dream is fading, but I disagree. The American dream is always there. What is wrong is people's attitudes. We created our opportunities; having a positive attitude and seeing life as a winner is key to being able to seize those opportunities and bring them to fruition. One of the first mistakes that people make is to try to be a CEO before they know what happens in the mailroom. To be truly successful, you should start at the bottom and work your way up. The second mistake people so often make is to look for a job without dressing for the part. Many also ask to be paid the same or more than an experienced person in the field. There are steps we all have to follow in order to get ahead.

The other issue that I hear people discussing all the time is discrimination. In my experience, I have never been discriminated against; on the contrary, I think is a social problem that some people create without thinking. For instance, many people look to live in certain communities – their communities – whether they are Hispanic, Asian, black or white. They think that to preserve their traditions and their customs, they have to live within that particular community. I think that is a mistake. Whoever chooses to live exclusively with their ethnic or cultural community is isolating – or discriminating – themselves from others. When you choose to live and integrate yourself with the overall community, you can be what you are, as long as you respect rules, regulations and bylaws. Everyone is equal.

The best advice that I can give anyone is to not start anything you cannot finish. Whether it is a project or the idea for an entire business, follow through and execute the idea. That's part of the positive attitude and passion. Secondly, if you are looking for a job, always look for a job that fulfills you or one that is related to whatever you are studying. Do not work simply to pay the bills, unless you enjoy being frustrated all the time. When you are not happy in your work, your performance suffers and you become a liability, instead of an asset, to that company. That is not good for anybody. As for me, I lasted less than a year in most of the jobs I had because I was constantly looking for a better opportunity. Importantly, however, I always left on good terms with every employer, and that meant the door would stay open to me, in case I needed their help someday. Build good relationships with employers, and they will open the door when you knock.

Here is something to think about: "The difference between, where you were yesterday and where you are going to be tomorrow is what you think, say, and do today."

Last but not least, usually some people ask for opportunities while others let opportunities pass them by. The truth of the matter is that in order to reach your goals in life, you have to create your own opportunities.

CHAPTER SEVEN

Running a Successful Small Business

"Many of life's failures are people who did not realize how close they were to success when they gave up."
G.K. Chesterton

In this chapter, I would like to discuss the basics of running a successful business. First of all, when one becomes a business owner, it is essential to thoroughly understand the line of business one is getting into. Unbelievably, many people fail to do that. As a result, they encounter problems and obstacles, and the business, instead of growing and becoming profitable, either scrapes by or fails.

When running a business, there are two critical things to keep in mind. In fact, they are the two most important things: growth and profitability. With smart marketing and networking, a business can only grow. And that business has to make money in order to succeed and grow. Of course, it goes without saying that ethics and first-class client service must also be part of any business scenario.

The insurance business, which is the business I chose to become part of 32 years ago, is an intangible product. It has a monumentally important function: to protect people's lives, homes and cars. But, as in many businesses, sales is a key component. Here are some rules I follow that have worked very well for my business:

- Keep the office neat and attractive
- Keep your own appearance neat and attractive
- Learn to listen
- Have a positive attitude
- Be aware of your body language
- Be confident
- Show courtesy at all times
- Always make eye contact
- Ask politely for referrals
- Once the sale is closed, send thank you notes.

The following gives you some insight into the system I created to help turn my agency into an income-producing machine:

First of all, create a system from day one. New business systems, cross sales systems, referral systems...all need to be developed and completely documented if they are going to turn your agency into a system dependent business.

Referral System

My agency lives on referrals. We don't just ask for referrals, we demand it. Using the Emergency Contact program, we get customers to give us at least 3 names of people we can contact in the event of a large catastrophic loss. Whether or not you live in an area that has catastrophes, it does not matter. The key here is to develop a system and make sure your employees stick to it.

Realtor Referral Program

I created my Realtor Referral Program early in my career and just started with 5 Realtors. In less than 10-years, I grew this network of realtors to over 80 active referral sources. In addition to the realtors, I networked with Title Companies and Mortgage Companies. Anyone that was involved in the home purchase was a target for us to go after.

The process worked like this:

- We call the potential customer; provide them with a quote and when they agree, we ask them to set up an appointment to meet with us. We encourage both the husband and the wife to come in to sign the necessary paperwork.
- When they arrive, we go over coverage options and answer all of the questions they may have. Most agents never take the time to meet with them and this gives us the chance to tell them how we are different from other agencies who may only care about closing a policy.
- Before they leave, we ask them about how they are going to pay off the mortgage if one of them were no longer here to pay the debt. Although most people do not like to think about death, it is a topic we feel very strongly about and we highly encourage them to protect their loved ones in this manner. We show the pros and cons of permanent life insurance vs. temporary and then show how Universal Life is a combination of the two. Most clients like the Universal Life concepts.
- We handle an average of 10 appointments per day with a closing ratio of 40%. If we do not close something at

that time, we place them in a file and follow-up with them at a later time.

Employee Structure

You have to have at least one person in your office handling your agency retention. Most agents focus on new business and fail to create systems to hold on to the business they have.

For every 500 policies-in-force (PIF), you need to have at least one employee to maintain your agency. If you want to grow, you need more. Invest in good people and reap the rewards.

Communication is Key

Follow up with your customers! Return phone calls quickly and make sure your staff does the same. Most customers leave you because you or your staff fails to return phone calls or explain price increases. Call your customers before they call you! Don't give them the chance to get a competing quote. If they love you, they will never call another company for a quote.

Goal Setting

Set high but achievable goals.

Incentivize Your Employees

What reason do your employees have to sell more policies or to treat your customers with the respect they deserve? Do you really know what goes on when you are not in the office? You may think you do, but do you really? Creating a reward system for you employees is crucial to your overall success! If you have it right, your employees will feel rewarded and will never ask for a raise. If they want to earn more, they know they have to create better results!

Share Your Vision

You may know what your agency is going to look like in 5 years, but does your staff? Share with them your vision for the agency and get them involved in creating programs to make your vision become a reality.

Take Responsibility for Your Own Success

As an agent, you own your own business – you need to stop acting like an employee and think like an owner. Good employees don't cost you money, they make you money. Spend money on things that are going to make you money. Great business owners know this and are always looking for new ways to increase revenue.

If times are tough, don't stop spending money on marketing!! That is a mistake I see new agents make all of the time. When times are tough, just get creative. Hire part-time employees, set goals, hold yourself and your staff accountable to reach your goals and make something happen every day!

Stay Positive

Surround yourself around positive people who bring you up, not bring you down. You know whom I'm talking about...the guy who always tries to sit by you in the meetings and complains about everything. That is the one you want to avoid at all costs.

CHAPTER EIGHT

Stress, Health and Happiness

"Every human being is the author of his own health or disease."
Buddha

Our health is the most precious thing we have, and we often take it for granted. I am one of those people. Building a business and a family, I was too busy to worry about my health. I had more important things to do. Or so I thought. Until the day I started having chest pains.

They lasted for a couple of hours, and then they got worse. That is when I went to the hospital. The doctors inserted a catheter and discovered that one of my arteries was 80 percent clogged. They cleaned it out and placed a stent inside it. Once the procedure was done and I knew I was going to be okay, I was relieved. But I wasn't same the person who loved to party and have fun. The possibility of my own mortality changed me. A year later, I found myself short of breath, so I went to my cardiologist, and he performed a carotid artery test. The test revealed that the right side of my carotid was clogged. From there, he sent me to talk to another doctor, who agreed to perform a carotid endarterectomy to remove the plaque in my artery. I checked into Methodist Hospital a few days before Christmas in 2006. About six hours after the surgery, I was taken to Intensive Care in terrible pain and unable to speak. The doctors gave me pain medicine, but when I woke up, I still couldn't talk. My surgeon reassured me that things would improve gradually and released me from the hospital on Christmas Eve.

Two months went by and still my voice was silent. I went back to Methodist Hospital to request my surgery records and got the surprise of my life. According to the papers filed, the surgeon of record was not my own surgeon but another doctor I didn't know. After four months with no voice and no response from my surgeon's office, I filed a lawsuit. A voice specialist examined me and said that the surgery had paralyzed a nerve in my right vocal cord, which was why I had lost my voice. That specialist then performed a surgery to try to reactivate the damaged nerve. After that procedure and extensive therapy, 80 percent of my voice returned.

After nearly two years in court, I won the lawsuit. But the doctor's attorney filed an appeal and won the case on that appeal. In my opinion, I lost the second time because no other doctor was willing to testify against one of their own and because the legal system seems to protect those who can afford to spend big money defending themselves. I spent around $10,000, but Perry Mason wasn't my attorney. The thing is, I wasn't trying to win big from this lawsuit; I wanted to show the Texas Medical Board what my doctor had done to me in allowing another doctor to perform surgery on me. Ultimately, what really mattered was that I had my voice again, and for that, I was grateful.

The reason for the title of this memoir, Meaningful, must be clear now. I always try to make sense of everything I do and I make a point of living life to the fullest. Anything and everything has to mean something for me to continue moving forward. I know now how short life is and can be, and I cherish every moment with those I love. To that end, here are a few morals to my own story:

> ROOTS. Those anchors that allow us to grow and develop. When you are raised the way I was raised, with a lot of love and guidance in my childhood, it creates very strong roots and offers a wonderful stability.

> VALUES. The ideals we establish for our lives.

> FRIENDSHIP. I have had many friends throughout my life, and with every relationship, I have learned many lessons, both good and bad. Among the most important has been about trust, and how it plays a starring role in what I consider real friendships.

> LOVE. A genuine emotion and feeling of warm attachment. With my wife, my children and grandchildren, I am surrounded of love in my life.

> PASSION. A very, very strong feeling. No matter what you do in life, you have to do it with passion or it's not worth the effort.

> ATTITUDE. A way of thinking, feeling or behaving that will lead to success.

> PERFECTION. The state of being without faults or flaws. Of course, nothing is perfect. But I nevertheless strive for perfection in everything I do, and the results over the years have been great.

> EDUCATION. The acquisition and development of knowledge and skill. Throughout my life, I have pursued education as the main ingredient to give flavor to my life.

Over the years along, my wife and I have had the opportunity to study and travel to many places around the world, where we have learned about other cultures, customs and ways of living. That has been an amazing education.

LEADERSHIP. The ability to lead. This is something that's part of my personality. I can't be a follower; I like to be the best at whatever I do.

BELIEF. To have faith. It's important to believe in yourself and your abilities to accomplish your objectives.

AWARENESS. Being conscious of everything at any moment.

RESPONSIBILITY. Accountability and obligation. When you commit to something in life, follow through on that commitment.

CULTURE. The tastes, manners and fashion that define us. When I was younger, I took classes in art and music for many years. From those, I learned the importance of refinement, elegance and politeness.

STRENGTH. The quality of being strong. Find out what your strengths are and develop them.

WEAKNESS. Those things you aren't good at doing. In my case, I don't like to talk in the phone, but I can deal with anybody in person or during a speaking engagement.

GOALS. That for which you make an effort. I am a goal setter in both my personal life and in business. For me, the most important thing is to get somewhere.

<u>OPPORTUNITY.</u>   An occasion to be seized. In soccer, there is a saying that "you will always miss 100 percent of the shots you don't take." That's also true in life because opportunities only come around once in a while. If you don't seize them, you will regret it.

<u>HURDLE.</u>   An obstacle or difficulty. Life will always throw obstacles in our way. The difference between a winner and a runner-up is in how we deal with them and keep moving forward.

<u>CHANGES.</u> Alterations or the means to become different. Life is all about changes. The important thing is to adjust to those changes as quickly as possible.

<u>DISCIPLINE.</u> A particular system of rules for conduct. This is the most important part to becoming a successful person.

<u>FOCUS.</u> Concentration. If you are going to be successful, you must be able to focus.

<u>ADVOCACY.</u> Speaking on behalf of something or someone. If you love what you do or the companies you work for, advocate for them.

<u>ACHIEVEMENTS.</u> Accomplishments. I have achieved much in my career because I put to work everything I talk about in this memoir.

<u>SUCCESS.</u> A favorable result. Here's what I tell my clients: "We can't spell 'success' without 'u'".

<u>THANKS.</u> An expression of gratitude. This is how I want to close, by expressing gratitude to all the people who have, in one way or another, helped and guided me.

Thank you for allowing me the opportunity to share my stories and experiences with you. I sincerely hope you picked up at least one idea that you can implement in your agency or in your life. If I can leave you with one idea or thought before you go, it is to live life every day as if it were your last. Live life with passion and purpose. The American Dream is yours if you believe in yourself and work hard.

I wish you and your family peace, love and happiness.

God bless you,

Gonzalo

A Collection of Art and Music

In this section, you will find some songs that I have written over the years as well as a few paintings. I hope you enjoy them.

BABY, YOU ARE THE ONE

AUTHOR: GONZALO JIMENEZ
COMPOSER: DANIEL ABADIA

DASVentures
L I M I T E D

Honorable Mention

This is to certify that

GONZALO JIMENEZ'S song

"BABY, YOU ARE THE ONE"

has been selected to receive an

Honorable Mention

in

The 2000 John Lennon Songwriting Contest

June 16, 2001

Brian Rothschild
Executive Director

The John Lennon Songwriting Contest

'ERES LA QUE YO AMO'

AUTOR: GONZALO JIMENEZ
COMPOSITOR: DANIEL ABADIA

DASVentures
L I M I T E D

Honorable Mention

This is to certify that

GONZALO JIMENEZ'S song

"ERES LA QUE YO AMO"

has been selected to receive an

Honorable Mention

in

The 2000 John Lennon Songwriting Contest

June 16, 2001

Brian Rothschild
Executive Director

The John Lennon Songwriting Contest

" BECAUSE OF YOU "

I want you to touch the sky ,with this moment
Let go your feelings, be yourself
Life is only one, enjoyed, live it
There is nothing that compares to you

I breath love, because of you
You fill me up always with your best
My life change for good , because of you
You made me, the way you want me to

Is because of you
That I just see beautiful tomorrows
Live beautiful today's
And see a bright future

I love the way you love
And your love makes me great
Your love does good to me
An is all because of you

My life is been a dream
That I never want to be awake
But If I wake up an open my eyes
It will be just to see you

I love the way you love
And your love makes me great
Your love does good to me
An is all because of you

" POR TI "

DESEO QUE CON ESTE MOMENTO, TOQUES EL CIELO
MUESTRA TUS SENTIMIENTOS, SE TU
SOLO HAY UNA VIDA, DISFRUTALA, VIVELA
NO HAY NADA QUE SE COMPARE A TI.

YO RESPIRO AMOR, POR TI
TU ME LLENAS SIEMPRE CON LO MEJOR
MI VIDA CAMBIO PARA BIEN, POR TI
TU ME HACES SER COMO TU QUIERAS QUE YO SEA.

ES POR TI
QUE YO VEO BELLOS MAÑANAS
VIVO BELLOS HOYS
Y VEO UN BRILLANTE FUTURO.

YO AMO LA MANERA COMO TU AMAS
Y TU AMOR ME HACE GRANDE
TU AMOR ME HACE BIEN
Y ES TODO POR TI.

MI VIDA A SIDO UN SUEÑO
QUE NUNCA DESEO SER DESPERTADO
PERO SI DESPIERTO Y ABRO MIS OJOS
SOLO SERA PARA MIRARTE A TI.

YO AMO LA MANERA COMO TU AMAS
Y TU AMOR ME HACE GRANDE
TU AMOR ME HACE BIEN
Y ES TODO POR TI.

A Simple Person

I am a simple person, with extraordinary luck, and when I say this, is because, there is few things that I am going to mentioned; that very few people accomplished and a lot of people do not appreciated.

First of all, I am in the best country in the world, which in my way of thinking, is the place to accomplish anything that you shut for.

Secondly, I am very honor to represent one of the best insurance companies and districts in United States.

Third, I am one of the best in the insurance business across the nation for many years, and remember I am a simple person, but with so much pride that I love to be the best in anything I do.

To my staff, only my respects, thanks guys.

In my personal life, I can tell you that 31 years ago I won the lottery, when I meet my wife Luz Marina which I love dearly, and she gave me 3 children that must of you know, that in one way or another are with our Farmers family, Jason, Bryan and Gina Lee, they are very successful in what they do and they are my life and pride. Also because of Luz I am where I am.

I was born in Bogota Colombia south America many years ago, when I left the country I was 17 years of age, and from that time on, " I DID IT MY WAY "

I been bless to know the right people in order to stablished my self in all business aspects, but you get this, being positive, having positive actituded at all times, And rejecting negative people in your lifes

Last but not least, I will recommended to everyone in district 65 including spouses or significant others, to keep doing what it works for you, and change effective now, what its not working in your business, don't be afraid, if you don't make this type of decisions today you will be sorry tomorrow, believe me I am very proud to see many agents changing for good and been successful, because they been applying my philosophy, " learn from others to enrich your self and allow people to know you for them to be successful as well"

One more thing, I thank God every day, for everything that happened to me and my family over the years having all of us together along with Luz family that for a long time, they are giving us the best of their lives helping us grow in our business, as Pablo Garcia, Nancy, Lady and Marcela, Eduardo Cubides, Nubia Garcia, and Jennifer Cubides, are doing over the years, Thank you guys from all of us.

Finally,Thru the years I learn so much from the Hastings family, Jeff, Brian, Laura; that the only thing that I can think at this moment is to say thanks everyone of you, for what you are and everything you do , I don't know anybody so much giving and caring without expecting anything, than Jeff, so my best advice to each and everyone in the district is to get aboard and play as a team for high performance, and you will see positive results.

GONZALO JIMENEZ

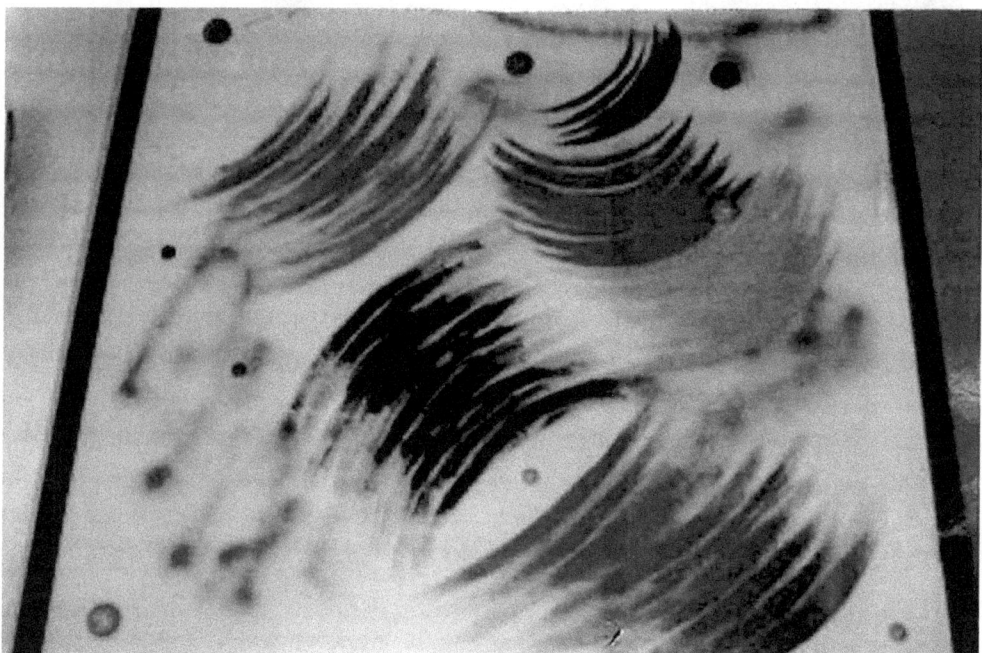

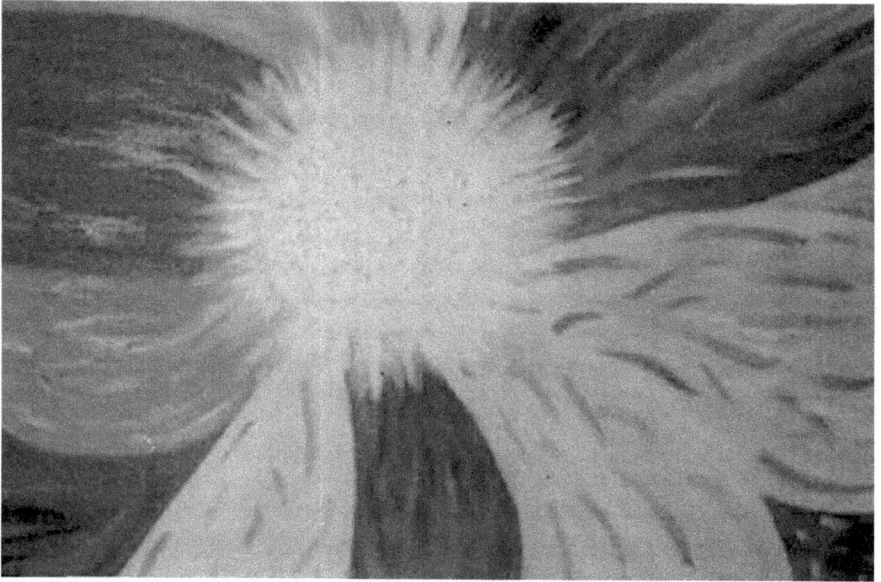

Agency Accomplishment

Life
Agent of the Year
Gonzalo Jimenez, *Sugar Land, Texas*

*Left to right: Paul Patsis,
Gonzalo Jimenez, Luz Marina Jimenez,
Martin D. Feinstein*

TO THE AUTHOR

Personally, there is no English or Spanish word to describe the fine and caring person that Gonzalo is. I have met many people in my life who, in some way, have helped me become a better person, but none like Gonzalo, who by example has shown me how to be a selfless, caring and giving individual. Thank you, Gonzalo, for sharing with me some of your experiences and knowledge that you have gained throughout the years, as this is truly a treasure that I devotedly cherish.

—Jorge Gonzalez, Jorge A. Gonzalez Insurance Agency

Gonzalo is a good friend, a wonderful person and a great leader in our community. He is a responsible person with unquestionable integrity and great character. Always inspiring me to move forward and try harder, he has encouraged me to keep spreading love, gratitude, and respect.

—Germán Cortés, Farmers Insurance Agent

I have known Gonzalo since I first became an agent in 1992. He is the same nice guy I met way back then. Gonzalo is the real deal. He is ready, willing and able to help anyone who asks him. He is a genuine good guy. He is consistent in his generosity and demeanor. His wife and kids are the same way. His legacy will continue on long after he is gone, God willing, many years from now! Gonzalo is an inspiration on how to live life to the fullest. I don't know how he does it. The man never seems to get tired. I am fortunate to call Gonzalo and his entire family friends!

—Bob Mitchell, Farmers Financial Solutions, LLC

Gonzalo is one of those unique individuals who stands and takes a challenge head on. He is not the most talented, or the smartest, or the best looking, but he is one of the most focused, honest, hard-working people I have ever known. Lillian and I have been proud to have known him and pray for his well-being. Thank you Gonzalo for the example you set, for so many.

—*Stephen Blakesley, GMS Talent LP*

Daddy, you are my hero and my rock. I am the woman I am today because of you. You have taught me to always hold my head up high and to be strong. I am the luckiest girl alive to have such a wonderful dad! I love you!

—*Gina Jimenez Garza*

Are you ready to take your agency to the next level?

Contact the Gonzalo Jimenez Agency for books, workshops and additional resources. At the Gonzalo Jimenez agency, it is our mission to help other achieve their goals and reach new heights. We've been helping insurance agents just like you live the American Dream and would love to work with you as well. Call us today for a free consultation.

Office: 713-270-0265
8323 Southwest Freeway, Suite 390
Houston, TX 77074

www.farmersagent.com/gjimenez

E-mail: gjimenez@farmersagent.com

Linked in.   www.linkedin.com/pub/gonzalo-jimenez

            @gjimenezagency

www.ingramcontent.com/pod-product-compliance
Lightning Source LLC
Chambersburg PA
CBHW060747100426
42813CB00032B/3426/J